UNCLE TIME

An International Poetry Forum Selection

It is time to plant
feet in our earth. The heart's metronome
insists on this arc of islands
as home.

Such an insistence does not, however, deny his intellectual
training. He knows, for example, that (as George Lamming
has put it) "English . . . is a West Indian language," and he
feels no embarrassment about making full use of it. He knows
also that Jamaican dialect is similarly available, and that for
some aspects of his experience it is more appropriate than
"Standard English" would be.

Scott takes a variety of approaches to the employment of
distinctively Jamaican language in his poems. In "Con-
struction," for example, the dialect voice is so presented as it
might accurately have been transcribed. There is meaningful
ambiguity in "de work sign" (the work has been signed; and/
or, the work's own signature) and also in "Now dat is hard"
(the brick has now dried out hard; and/or, now that is diffi-
cult). But the poem depends mainly on the power of the idea
in the last four lines to suggest the mystery of creation. In the
elegy "Grampa" and in "Uncle Time" there is a literary
heightening of the dialect, perhaps most noticeably in "When
I was four / foot small," "that old molasses / man," and—
in "Uncle Time"—"smile black as sorrow." Just as Standard
English is, the dialect is manipulated and modified for the
artist's particular purpose.

"Standard English" is, of course, a flexible concept allow-
ing for a fair range of local variation; there is Jamaican Stan-
dard English, though we might argue about what qualifies.
Dennis Scott moves freely between words and structures
which are internationally current and usages which are more
or less local. In "Nightflight," for example, an echo of *Othello*
("put out each light / and then put out / the moon rising")

xix

leads almost immediately into a Jamaican idiom, "and everything / quiet" (everything is quiet). Coming upon "No sufferer" the non-Jamaican reader should be aware of the concentration in "like the fires behind your fences" (where the fires are also emotional, and the fences have multiple significance, including skirmishes, pretenses, protective barriers). But he will hardly recognize the sophistication with which the poem involves the local life and language of black Jamaicans, particularly the Rastafarians, in presenting the mind of its persona.

In current Jamaican usage, "sufferer" means not just anyone who suffers but primarily someone who is black and poor. The Rastafarians believe that the black man in Jamaica is far away from his African home, which, unhistorically, the Rastafarians place in Ethiopia. "Version" is the term used for an instrumental rendering of a vocal pop record, often sold as the flip side of the hit on a 45 rpm disc. Insistent Rastafarian drumming can be heard as comforting; for the group around the drum it expresses their communal longing for Africa. To a Jamaican, "ratchets" suggests the ratchet knife, a weapon mainly of the underprivileged. "Dread," a complex word in Rastafarian usage, suggests cool anger, a sort of menacing stillness. "Chains" recalls us, of course, to the conditions of slavery which transported blacks from Africa. "Mabrak" is "black lightning," a Rastafarian concept.

A great deal is compressed in "acknowledge I." Rastafarians often use "I" for both nominative and accusative. "I" seems to assert the sanctity of the individual but also implies the community of "I and I" (first person plural). Scott's "acknowledge I" has many significances, including "I acknowledge," "acknowledge me," "acknowledge my Rastafarian brothers." So the poem, having maintained a tension between the persona's denial that he is a sufferer (in the material sense) and his eagerness to establish emotional identity with Rastafarian suffering, comes to rest with a reverence so expressed as to complete the fusion.

Scott's compassion is no more restricted than his language. It reaches out to the domestic servant whose "mouth has eaten the unleavened bread / of yes ma'am, no ma'am, in a place of salt." "Squatter's rites" mourns the death of a derelict Rastafarian "king of a drowsy hill . . . scratching his majesty / among the placid chickens." The persona in "Pages from a Journal, 1834" is a white man going home to England from Jamaica, saying "good-bye to dark: / These black clowns and their manacled capers," yet haunted by his memories of Jamaica, "inked . . . and hard to erase": "only the past permits / no unchaining." "Farmer's Notebook" is critical of "our cutlasses, blood-drunk," "our hate," and obviously concerned for the decapitated white woman whose "head startles / the children"; though, as the poem is written from the point of view of one of the blacks, the effect is complicated. Adopting the first person plural, the persona shares responsibility for the inhumanity he condemns. With bitter irony ("They hanged him on a clement morning"), "Epitaph" laments the death of a slave, but seems to suggest that anger is an easier, less appropriate response than reverent regret.

In the "Black Mass" sequence (written while he was in Athens, Georgia), Scott further explores black-white relationships and restates a human need:

> But I am haunted by your occasional grace, and I will
> not relinquish
> that dim voice from the singing in my head
> though the black dead and white stand between us
> it is time to praise
> whatever after such killing will make us kind.

In that poem, "Recessional," Caroline seems to represent white culture (a "white" muse?) as well as white flesh.

Such poems help define Scott's attitudes as a black Jamaican artist. He is concerned about the inequalities of his society, he knows black people suffer, and he knows that he is black; but his compassion will not be limited, his human sympathies are wide. As a poet he must deliver the poems that come, and this is no easy task:

> There is a beak at the back of his throat—
> the poem is difficult,
> his tongue bleeds.

A great many of Scott's poems are, at least in part, about the nature of the creative act; some less obviously so than others. Take, for example, "The Dumb-School Teacher":

> Words had shapes
> changeable as
> aspects of the truth
> they learned,
> talking of grief and glory
> with the same quick palms.

Or "Private," a love poem in which the woman seems to shade into a muse.

In "For the Last Time, Fire" Scott tackles values opposed to the imagination:

> The phoenix hid at the sun's center and stared down
> at the Banker's house,
> which was plump and factual, like zero.
> Every good Banker knows
> there's no such bird.

Yet he does not deny the reality of the ordinary world in which a phoenix is unthinkable. His imagination confronts and uses a "real" world of history, present social conditions, personal relationships; he writes movingly about love, parting, death. The persona in "Solution" is impelled to murder a killer, then

Slowly the eye heals. Weary of watching murder, it dissolves,
    it invents
dream

But "dream," the world of Scott's imagination, is not some tranquil retreat. It is a testing place:

> In the stone gardens of my mind
> there are old men with fingers like scissors,
> snip, snip. Harvesting heads.

MERVYN MORRIS
University of the West Indies,
Kingston, Jamaica

UNCLE TIME

~ Bird of Passage

The poet is speaking.
The window reflects his face.
A bird crawls out of the sun. Summoned.
Its wings are like tar.
That is because it is very hot.
The poet sweats too.
There is a beak at the back of his throat—
the poem is difficult,
his tongue bleeds.
That is because the bird is not really
dead. Yet.
Clap a little.

~ Infidelities

Two boys battle on a flat, green field,
outside the village. At noon, when my sister
brings them thick, flaked flour-cakes
and her water-cool voice, both will yield.

There are no more dragons to fight to the death,
and young hearts are hot as the leaping sun;
that is why, and because she has smiled at one,
they shiver the gay air with their breath.

How jealous they are! How vainly they fight!
I watch the dark brown boys and laugh;
my sister is safe; when boys, at night,
in these islands, dream, their dreams are white.

◦ Exile

There is a kind of loss,
like coming home
to faces; the doors open in-
differently; they whisper,
"Who is this, with dust
in his mouth? Who
is this new traveler?
Tell us of birds,
migrating the dull sky
half a world round,
of Ithaca, and the tiered beast,
of that foreign city
you sent your pale card from!"

There are patterns to assure us:
at table, familiar spices;
the garden, hardly greener;
but something has changed:
clothes we left behind;
the old affections hang loosely.
Suddenly, mouth is dumb; eyes
hurt; surprised, it is we
who have changed; glad, now,
to have practiced loving
before that departure. To travel
is to return
to strangers.

∾ Homecoming

The wind is making countries
in the air, clouds dim,
golden as Eldorado voyages.
                    Those hills
harbor a sea of dreams, they told
us; and as children we were
sad, wanting a rainbow.
                    Now
heart-sailed
from home I name them
Orient, Africa,
New York, London's white
legend; the ports have
a welcoming ring—no end
to their richness, their tumble.
The sirens sing.
                    But

again, again these
hot and coffee streets reclaim
my love. Carts rumble.
The long horn of a higgler's voice
painting the shadows midday
brown, cries about harvest,
and the wind calls back
blue air across the town; it tears
the thin topographies of dream, it blows me
as by old, familiar maps,
to this affectionate shore, green
and crumpling hills,
like paper in the Admiral's fist.
The rain comes down.

                    There is a kind of tune
we must promise our children,
a shape that the quadrant measures,

no North
to turn them
away from the dissonant cities,
the salt songs,
the hunger of journeys.

It is time to plant
feet in our earth. The heart's metronome
insists on this arc of islands
as home.

ᕲ Visionary

One great wing marks his shoulder;
that's why he stumbles
headlong against the sun;
the stuttering wind
bears him
unevenly
across air; wounded
and willful he
beats to home,
one arm shielding
his eyes from
the sun's gold flower,
the hills folding back
under his journey, the stubborn,
heavy pounding of that
one wing wonderful. Not quite
can earth recall him,
Icarus, this brave
limping bird, making
such fierce way
to a hoped-for home: wise
and wandering with the sun
grown in his eyes.

◇ *Precautionary Measures*

On certain days
the old house thunders open, the field
shivers its flat side like damp horses,
when crust cracks away from
wall, hair, wood's black,
the sun

trickles like a slow stone
into the rooms of my head
along wind
transparent and drifting. Everything is
shaped, is liquid, is
finished. The sun
wanders like stormseed
full and heavy between
the furniture of grief.

I cover that mirror
with scarves of silence and rainbow
lest the sky break

and discover
an old man
chopping the trees down
making a green smell for his hands
and his glittering voice.

⌇ Portrait of the Artist as a Magician

He painted the ball
first, balancing on it himself
a pale boy soft as young thorns,
and in his hand mirrors.
In these he observed
a delicate equilibrium.
Then all around, the details of such a summer
as he had known, the sun too, for that
to age as it would
the sturdy tree lifting to it.
At each stroke he cried out. (This may have been ecstasy.)

When it was entirely there, reflecting
something of what was true,
he applied white. The picture snowed out.

But the ball began to roll, making a neat black frame
        around the figure, everything
began to roll

ᔫ Sentry

It is forbidden to sleep on guard.
In the dreamshadow you can't see them limping along,
    covering their baskets like mouths.
Besides that, stone frosts and must be kept dry, or
    it shivers to sand,
things have a tendency to liquefy; become old
in the darkness of anger, running away into crevices.
Nobody explained this to me when I came.

Only I noticed the muscles softening, the flesh
    creased and ripened,
the young faces pinched
off at the base, breaking like shy stalks.
Since then I watch against reapers.

In the stone gardens of my mind
there are old men with fingers like scissors,
snip, snip. Harvesting heads.

⌒ Construction

Some time in de greathouse wall
is like a thumb mark de stone,
or a whole han.
Granny say is de work sign, she say
it favor when a man tackle de stone, an' mek
to tear it down, till de mortar tek de same shape
as him han. But I feel say
is like sumaddy push de wall up
an' hole it dere until de brick dem dry
out. Now dat is hard.

～ Work in Progress: For E.M.

You can see in
the grain of her hands' bone, carved
like Dürer or the prayers of country women
accustomed to hard, simple things.
They have stripped down the flesh to essentials:
    pain, patience,
a capacity for sunlight. When she covers her eyes
smiling, the horses tremble
against a closed curve of lid,
longing for meadows.

But when she is finished
and the wood stained by silence
(appearance of sorrow,
condition of angels),
she will lead them out with bridles of hair,
all white laughter; her face
shattered by those kind hooves.

～ Fisherman

The scales like metal flint his feet,
their empty eyes like me.
How gray their colors in the heat!
Cool as the oily sea.

With gentle hands he slits the heart,
and the flesh as white as milk
and the ribboned entrails fall apart
like the fall of coiling silk.

Some day I too shall fish, and find
on stranger shores than these
the ribs and muscles of my blind
self, rainbowed from the seas.

~ Because of the Cats

Because of the cats, no dreams
because I know how the moon
strikes fire on their flint eyes
how their rank smells excite them
because I remember challenge and the low crawl
the coil and creep of thin sinew
over brick, this room
is a stone tomb, I wish
to be king too, fluid as those sovereigns
melting past my window, spilling
like shadows past the garbage pans
and the almond tree
crying my lust from yard to yellow moon;
I am torn from sleep,
tongue shivers and arches to call
"I am coming" my skin moves
my fur folded against the sheets.
I am coming, brothers!
A white howl slashes the night
like a painted hunger.
There are bars on my window.

Listen! No dreams tonight
they are calling past the restless dogs,
past the brown streets and the zinc fences—
something wild in me wakes
wants to be free, my nails scratching
the cold bed's iron, something old
shakes the door on its hinges
like a breath of wind
that some soft arrogant beast turns
in my bed, snarls in my egg-skull
cracks my eye staring to the pale window
where my brothers spit
and the cool sharp moon slices
my padded feet like broken screams
because of the cats.

～ Nightflight

One evening we hunted
fireflies, laughing
to see the rain
put out each light
and then put out
the moon rising, and all of us
went home, and everything
quiet.

Tonight great bats dragged in
with a velvet hunger
spiraling drunk to the sweet rot below.
Basking, they floated
staring at the hot, white moon
blindly. Squealed, shook the wet splashing
air down through trees
and came to the feast.
Now, everything quiet.

Except the slow rain slanting
on the roof, chanting
a childhood rhyme I cannot
exorcise, except
the bright fruit falling
into my sleep from time
to time, like fireflies.

He made them books,
turning the leaves
of his hands
like old, cracked testaments;
between the lines
they read his love.
Words had shapes
changeable as
aspects of the truth
they learned,
talking of grief and glory
with the same quick palms.
And what a gossip in the eye,
what a babble
of necessary, sleight-
of-hand!

So when he died
they spoke of his folded
lips in whispers,
making no distinction
between prayers at his passing
and their talk of weather
and wonder. He most of men
they knew
found endless praise
in the silence of their chatter
their moving hands
his monument.

~ Majesty

The golden brute
walks into my blood
like an aristocrat. He scratches the mask,
the fool whimpers,
he idles through the cracks of that face,
the shadows are blue
where his eye has gone, he is
the brain's design.
The court enters, stunned with indigo,
they abase themselves,
he is moody and consolate
(the dead break off their branches for him, the bones
extend fruit for his tongue.
He purrs.) Aiee!
Who will cage him
in the weird of the flesh, who will entertain him?

～ House

Somebody left me
this house. I
came to it meaning to stay.

One morning I noticed
how sad
it was, soiled and familiar.
That day

nobody came.
The summer game was over.

Well, I shan't move
till I have to,

if you're careful and play
possum inside you don't hardly notice
the smell of the horses. Only sometimes

the blood forgets. Then I ride
my sleep through the snuffling house
like wind, their shoes crack
fire from the windows,
the windows are shaking, RATATAT
the front door bangs open

and shut, slowly. I glimpse
road outside, and the changing

positions of sunlight.

⌒ At that frail and absent evening house,

something glitters. She is waiting.
She sings from her open cage.
Each note snaps another rose.
It splinters.
Every splinter contains a reflection.
Between them her shadow shuffles,
a slow dance. The long day
has cut trenches in her voice.
That is why the garden is breaking.
There are sharp blue lines round her mouth.
It is possible to enter there and be immediately lost.
The crystal stems make a forest of thorns.
Raked, I go carefully
in.

The suddentree has begun to bloom, killing
whatever passes.
Whipping birds out of the air.
A sad horse chokes on its own mane.
That man is covered with flowers, and he won't ever wake.

Only you remain
casual under its shadow, untouched,
closing your skin to its sharp, fragrant leaves,
forbidding the nourishment of grief to that terrible root.

I have seen you lift from its hollow combs of honey.

～ Dive

When your hand stumbled against my face, the cage
opened,
the blood spun away, separating. Everything
which was not simple unclouded
the eye. That slammed shut.
The skull was full of clear water
for you.

It was a long, dry journey.
Then your face broke
like stone. I fell to it
immediately, as if wingless, turning
to sleep through that slow river of your mouth. Ah.

(How quietly the drowned birds talk together.)

ᦐ The Compleat Anglers

Trolling for love
without deceit was difficult.
The starfish of our hearts
become dry and sharp
when we take off our bodies, sometimes,
going into the sea.
The sun is unforgiving.

We were at first so
afraid, careful, away from
the safety of flesh; I remember
your questions carved fish
in the nightwall, the sunken gallery
was alive on a sudden with hiding,
finny, hard to catch;
I drew a line
along your mouth, your hand,
and caught doubt.

Now when tides ebb
out to the whisper of deep water
we say true things
or drift in silence, trusting that
away from the incontinent shore
we may come suddenly on
shoals of kindness.

The doors are unnumbered,
most of them open
into your face.

One is house. Day begins at
that bed. And ends there.
I remember that.

And there. The classroom where I learn
things, other people.
Your voice only schools me to silence.

This door is locked. I hear
the cold inside. Sometimes
I pass it slowly.

A cry, very soft. Or the wind.
You are here
too.

～ Rainsong: For W. K.

You touch her: and rain scratches like feet
at the ceiling. They are playing their gray and pitiless
      games
above her bed. The rain is filling her mouth. Beware,
she will drown.
      Be wise; talk little of love—
they will nibble your voice, they will shred your laughter.
      Fondle her
gently—their small teeth have tattered
the quicks of your fingers.
Feed her your dreams, applesweet—
they will foul that white flesh too
like blood gone old, staining the wall
brown.

Only the perfectly circular twining of silence will bring
      rest. It alone will hold
dry leaves of love over her, though they finally fall,
      gathered
into that nest the rats' dark copulation weaves
under the scampering eaves.
The rainsong hums down.

◌ The Separation

The scratched moon, maybe.
That's how high she jumping
hung by her breaking nails
slid screaming
through the afternoon's long death
down its flat white mercy
in slow motion, gone
away, gone away

and I have gone
between the evening streets
sucked thin by the cracked air,
called, my voice of rain
between the walled and serpent streets
hanging my cries like animals
among the metal trees, their bark
rusts at her name; and
one there is furry with her
hair, it's caught
where a branched fist
tore at her skull
to keep her till I came
but leaping terribly she
combed herself free,
going violent and high
from the sharp hills' attraction, falling
away, away down, forgetting
she would fall
never making a sound
forever away from
the pure moon's circle
from the moon's rough round,
turning over and over

unable to sleep. Or to hide.
And in the early morning
at last, I dreamed

I came where she had died
behind a falling fence,
zinc and starlight,
a patchwork thing
of screams, her mouth
torn open. The thick sea
in it drifted a shape
astonished as the clear, flat moon
on her tongue, on her tongue,
floating like some white
and incredible sacrament
on the warm, salt scum of her
blood. My face.

ᵔ Cotyledon

Slowly as seed dissolves
into something green and pliant
I am
forgetting the stretch of your body across
my arm the weight of
your eyes taking mine, giant
spaces, where your hollows hold me.
It's a small cold thing
this cotyledon of no you
this lonely of your absence.

I am forgetting
the presentations of your laughter;
I fill my hands with echoes
not hair not here any
more than usual friendships. Light,
tenderly, time encourages
a hard going a
way of pain. Night

is the terrible time
for lying, the seed
in my head too big for sleep
green tendrils of my breath
crawl from the mouth.
I am forgetting

how carefully this growing
imitates death.

～ The Reunion

More than the blood's leap they expected
(though knowledgeable in love's transcience)
more even than the difficult, neglected
language, like a strange tongue after absence,

this surprised them: that their shadows lay
longer and longer, quicker than they
having no fear, nothing to say,
growing together, then fading away

as they left the certain lights behind
like streetlamps; moving from the pain
of bright remembrance to the tender, blind
treacheries of being together again.

∽ Celebrating,

my brother the worm
has no voice
but he comes and goes, comes and

not until the seed has shocked open
and dislodged the stone, the smallest lace of leaf.
But then that spear leaps as fiercely
as I love you, justifying
the halves of my head, gut. And naturally

soon there will be most delicate patterns of vein
suitable for his hunger. In the silence between us
I hear his impatience, the clatter of earth
on your eyes.

∽ Uncle Time

Uncle Time is a ole, ole man. . . .
All year long 'im wash 'im foot in de sea,
long, lazy years on de wet san'
an' shake de coconut tree dem
quiet-like wid 'im sea-win' laughter,
scraping away de lan' . . .

Uncle Time is a spider-man, cunnin' an' cool,
him tell yu: watch de hill an' yu se mi.
Huhn! Fe yu yi no quick enough fe si
how 'im move like mongoose; man, yu tink 'im fool?

Me Uncle Time smile black as sorrow;
'im voice is sof' as bamboo leaf
but Lawd, me Uncle cruel.
When 'im play in de street
wid yu woman—watch 'im! By tomorrow
she dry as cane-fire, bitter as cassava;
an' when 'im teach yu son, long after
yu walk wid stranger, an' yu bread is grief.
Watch how 'im spin web roun' yu house, an' creep
inside; an' when 'im touch yu, weep. . . .

So, good-bye to dark:
These black clowns and their manacled capers,
that brooding of hills. We sail
at dusk, taking the tide out
by the moon's chronometer.
The island floats behind
me not leaving,
dragging itself in the ship's road by
a seaweed cord.
The deck smells
of sugar and spices, spiders breed
their scuttling memories in
the green stems
below, the Captain tells me;
and below, I am glad to be gone—

                  yet

the hills are woodcut wild,
inked at my heart
and hard to erase;
to the last I possess them,
their branches, their sun,
the carved black dancers—
I have printed myself
their wooden glances
with an iron pride
more savage than theirs.
I have signed them.

The paper darkens
away from that porthole moon,
a fistful of wind
bellies us north-northeast;
turn in. The spiders
throw their silk across the hold,
the turning fruit prepare
a tropic gold. Perhaps
when London snows
I shall be sad
buying their sweet
splendor, to recall
the green remaining.
Sea knots slip
apart; only the past permits
no unchaining.

∿ All Saints

Like a tongue shivering
at the wind's throat
the hill moves a little.
In the chapeled grass,
an introit of birds.

Today the walls of libraries
break open, bird shadows
pierce the shelves and disfigure
the pages. In offices too
desks are charred
by the energy of our desire;
in the houses we leave
machines open—
mouthed, wounded; idols
are shaken to dust, the theaters
crack like eggs
in sunlight, revealed
as mockeries, imprecise.
No need for darkness now
to contain the hatched wings' thrust.

We leave the city
pursued by memories
drawn towards the pocked hill.

Do not expect marble
or epitaphs. We will
recognize their rooms
by the sound of grass
over them. We arrive.

Those who remember
begin with laughter,
asserting the perpetual
delight of makers:
>what I say is true
>what I say is true
>as these witness.

And softly, as a hill survives,
resisting the weight of grass, wind, sunstroke,
as birds compose
voluntaries in air
after a yolked, hard beginning,
we rehearse
their acts of endurance,
we perform
their freedom,
making confession:
>in the violence of our coming
>this place has possessed us
>this place has possessed us
>all who came
>victor and victim
>its possession.

Till the old ones, chained and rooted
in their ribbed chancels
are comforted by our devotion,
the great birds hurled
and rejoicing like requiems up
the arching wind,
the hill's green motion.

~ Grampa

Look him. As quiet as a July river-
bed, asleep, an' trim' down like a tree.
Jesus! I never know the Lord could
squeeze so dry. When I was four
foot small I used to say
Grampa, how come you t'in so?
an' him tell me, is so I stay
me chile, is so I stay
laughing, an' fine
emptying on me—

laughing? It running from him
like a flood, that old molasses
man. Lord, how I never see?
I never know a man could sweet so, cool
as rain; same way him laugh,

I cry now. Wash him. Lay him out.

I know the earth going burn
all him limb dem
as smooth as bone,
clean as a tree under the river
skin, an' gather us
beside that distant Shore
bright as a river stone.

∿ Resurrections

There's nothing delicate

about this tree they chopped.
The blunted bole has healed
a makeshift gray. Each day
the rain applies its poultices
of dust. Patient, it seems,
it seems—

         and nothing tender in her mouth.
Her mouth has eaten the unleavened bread
of yes ma'am, no ma'am, in a place of salt.
One of her men died
in a war, three more at birth,
one from a tree—fell down;
so she fell down again
each Sunday at the mercy seat,
sang hymns of healing
as she swept the floor. Waiting for rain.

And one day soon she won't be
out to work. Sick.
She's been bred; the gardener
chopped her into life, they say.
No wasted glory,

         but with sudden flesh
the tree empties its longing to the light
invincible, and green.

～ Kindergarten

My father the farmer's
hard at work into dusk.
He stoops against the darkness, patiently
stabbing flowers, weeds, down
to let the young trees grow.

He's buried snail-shell, beetle, calyx, buttercup seed
under that gray hair too;
the skin peeled off would show
veined leaves rotting
like moss between the follicles,
small glories pared away, Christmas-candlesticks burnt
and forked under.
You pay for what you plant.

Now knowing a familiar rustle, he turns,
the rope of his mouth's muscle dredging up, dragging up
a memory of laughter to his face.
I watch myself grow
at his cornea, taking shape in
his mind

(but the blue-dusk light lies,
like water: I am no longer smooth
limbed, supple, but rough and refractive
as by wind
after absence from your fences)

yet here for a moment
my hand roots to his shoulder
against the world's bare weather;
I am moved by that habit of flesh
and affection, taking
my half-forgotten place
beside him, like any other green, obedient thing.

The canes burn. I show you
a vision of smoke: poled high,
cut, her head startles
the children; birds die crisply
among our cutlasses, blood-drunk
shriveled smaller than her tongue.
Perhaps it is the heat
she complained of. Year after year

I remember her
rings, heavy as iron,
and the great linen sails
of her gown's passage. Hoisted now,
her yellow hair silent
she stares home
past our hate, through
the ash falling like gray wind on her
mouth, loose in the shimmering air.

And when the field furls out later
its emerald knives,
will you forget that
thick flesh here, grown
soft and nourishing?

∽ Epitaph

They hanged him on a clement morning, swung
between the falling sunlight and the women's
breathing, like a black apostrophe to pain.
All morning while the children hushed
their hopscotch joy and the cane kept growing
he hung there sweet and low.
                    At least that's how
they tell it. It was long ago
and what can we recall of a dead slave or two
except that when we punctuate our island tale
they swing like sighs across the brutal
sentences, and anger pauses
till they pass away.

~ Squatter's Rites

Peas, corn, potatoes; he had
planted himself
king of a drowsy hill; no one
cared how he came to
such green dignity,
scratching his majesty
among the placid chickens.

But after a time, after
his deposition, the uncivil wind
snarled anarchy through that
small kingdom. Trees, wild birds
troubled the window,
as though to replace the fowl
that wandered and died of summer;
spiders locked the door,
threading the shuddered moths,
and stabbed their twilight needles through
that gray republic. The parliament of dreams
dissolved. The shadows tilted
where leaf-white, senatorial lizards
inhabited his chair.

Though one of his sons made it,
blowing reggae (he
dug city life)
enough to bury the old Ras
with respect
ability and finally,
a hole in his heart;
and at night when the band played
soul, the trumpet
pulse beat
down the hill
to the last post,
abandoned,

leaning in its hole
like a scepter
among the peas, corn, potatoes.

～ Report on the Possibility of Effecting
Some Kind of Change Next Week

1. Sunday: when the Chairman entered
everyone fell
down, recovering simplicity
at the round table. The grail
lit up, flashing lights,
gave a time signal.
There were many reporters,
their questions shaking like loose leaves,
fluttering. The interview began.

2. Monday: we are all equal,
said the Chairman. But I am
concerned to note how
the commune is betrayed.
Some leave early, distributing
silences over our faces.
"What shall we do
when the bread comes to an end?"

3. Tuesday: the carmeras circle him slowly.
The Chairman diets and is friendly to his people
The Chairman makes few appearances today
The Chairman is sorely tried
The Chairman is tired
the cameras circle him slowly.
What's the hurry, we ask,
what's the hurry.
Is there some place
is there some special meeting to attend.

4. Wednesday: like a great stem
the steering rod
bloomed him softly
when the assassins rammed
him leaving
his large whitehouse. National disaster:
CITIZEN UNDER
ARREST

5. Thursday: our leader the Chairman is
elegant. He's stopped speaking
the truth, since then he lies
in state. His constitution won't be
amended now; he's gone
out of business. Startlingly,
a boutonnière bleeds on his morning coat.

6. Friday: LONG LIVE THE CHAIRMAN!

7. Saturday: the car has been repaired and
repainted, the house shines every evening, new
flowers in the vases, dancing,
the bakers are working overtime.

8. Sunday: when the Chairman entered,
everyone fell
down, recovering.

⌢ For the Last Time, Fire

That August the birds kept away from the village, afraid:
        people were hungry.
The phoenix hid at the sun's center and stared down
        at the Banker's house,
which was plump and factual, like zero.
Every good Banker knows
there's no such bird.

She came to the house like an old cat, wanting
a different kind of labor.
But the Banker was busy, feeding his dogs, who were nervous,
Perhaps she looked dangerous.
The child threshed in her belly
when she fell. The womb cracked, slack-lipped,
leaving a slight trace of blood on the lawn. Delicately,
the phoenix placed the last straw on its nest.

Mrs. So-and-so the Banker's wife beat time
in her withdrawing room. Walked her moods
among the fluted teacups, toying with crusted foods.
The house hummed Bach, arithmetic at rest.
The phoenix sang along with the record,
and sat.
But the villagers counted heads, and got up.

So, logical as that spiral worming the disc to a hole in
        the center,
one night there were visitors, carrying fire. The dogs
        died first.
then they gutted everything.

Something shook itself out of the ash.
Wings. Perhaps.

～ Endgame

Caroline, bored and brooding,
watches them play on
the squared country.
An easy opening: the pawns forgotten to the wooden box
like root-stumps. Imagine
Winter.
      She lingers behind his castle
not understanding the game,
what will happen when

a horse's shadow runs, falls along
the straight cracks of that field.
In a moment it will turn, too swift
to deflect, the great carved feet arcing down
to his grinned skull, split as by spring,
the crown bladed, the mind
open and fat.
A bishop watches patiently. How
she will scream!

Black to move.

Here, if I stayed too
long, the skin would tear, scrawling
my viscera like smoking ropes, roads,
between the towns of the South.

                                    Caroline
swings on a sultry afternoon, sipping lemonade.
It keeps her cool. The sharp drink peels her smooth and
            pale.
Where did she find that rope?

There is a dark, dry man at the back door waits
holding his belly open, crying. Later, night
will lead her in to supper.

Unless he becomes impatient.

Hurry, Caroline, hurry. He is coming.

Is it time yet?

ᵔ Black Mass: Invitation

Evening. She fades, all frost,
into the poorer part of town; my shadow
jumps
her nervous promenade. The street burns maple, leaf-
sharp in carbon lights. Pretzel bones hunch her along
through Autumn, tilt and lunge
like old magnolia. She breaks against the wind.

Where are you going, Lady?
                                        I would waltz you
less crookedly to April if you'd have me,
but you mistake my love.
I'd melt you whole again, straight
out from ice-dream, from the terror of this blue
cold, my palm, from the twist of your desire into
bloom again—away from fire. Ah Caroline.
Winter's a comin in
3/4 time.
And you mistake my love.

We shall arrive at the set place soon.

It is time for the healing.
When the neophyte enters drumfall
muffles her whiteness. Torchlight softens the flesh
                in anticipation.
The motionless rain makes a pure dream of her dread.
                Of the knife,
the fire, the bowl. All that is needed
here. This
is winter. There is no way to arrive at resurrection
save through such approximate ecstasy.

Do not remove the skin. Go directly into
the cage. (The fountain will plume for a moment, staining
                your silence. The bowl will contain it.)
Drink.
Then the engine is taken out, still
hot. Close the wound with your affectionate hands.
Divide it between you.

It is for those who abstain from such communion that we
                provide
the fire.

I came on you at sunrise, putting out the flesh,
and cried too; some of them were mine.
Count the burned men, Lady. Count what remains.

Can these bones live?

But I am haunted by your occasional grace, and I will
    not relinquish
that dim voice from the singing in my head
though the black dead and white stand between us

it is time to praise
whatever after such killing will make us kind—
what patches us, melting
the shredded light back to itself
without fire
            Prism. This is the jewel
hooked at the mind's edge (all night their hands
clawed to that shape. Or offered it.)
                            And its magnificence
    will not be mocked
by talk of forgiving. It cannot decline, at the heart
    of flame
it is full, it explodes, containing us all
into the constant ceremonies of our living.

You in your Winter grief and I in mine.

∽ Solution

Small fish throttle
home at low tide; above, the gull is falling
intently. Falls a long time. Cataracts
down the eye. The claw scars
white into the retina. The feet
are stiff, its head hurls out, the hectic air chills, freezes,
cracks. Flensed,
the eye spills.

Night.

But at the moment of its arrival, when
the slashed eye is widest
the fish swing under, slung deep by the tide,
the clashed air closes safely behind them.
Nothing. The bird shrugs up
out of the sea. Then over

the tide my hand across
the wheeling air across
time and salt and the dunes of sorrow, look—I stretch, I am
      reaching
out, I
wrench its wings into stillness
I blunt that mouth
the hard feet break like straw.

Slowly the eye heals. Weary of watching murder, it dissolves,
      it invents
   dream

⌒ No sufferer,

but in
the sweating gutter of my bone
Zion seems far
also. I have my version—
the blood's drum is
insistent, comforting.
Keeps me alive. Like you.
And there are kinds of poverty we share,
when the self eats up love
and the heart smokes
like the fires behind your fences, when my wit
ratchets, roaming the hungry streets
of this small flesh, my city

: in the dread time of my living
while whatever may be human chains me
away from the surfeit of light, Mabrak
and the safe land of my longing,
acknowledge I.

Pitt Poetry Series

Adonis, *The Blood of Adonis*

Jack Anderson, *The Invention of New Jersey*

Jon Anderson, *Death & Friends*

Jon Anderson, *Looking for Jonathan*

Gerald W. Barrax, *Another Kind of Rain*

Fazıl Hüsnü Dağlarca, *Selected Poems*

James Den Boer, *Learning the Way*

James Den Boer, *Trying to Come Apart*

Norman Dubie, *Alehouse Sonnets*

John Engels, *The Homer Mitchell Place*

Abbie Huston Evans, *Collected Poems*

Gary Gildner, *Digging for Indians*

Gary Gildner, *First Practice*

Michael S. Harper, *Dear John, Dear Coltrane*

Michael S. Harper, *Song: I Want a Witness*

Samuel Hazo, *Blood Rights*

Samuel Hazo, *Once for the Last Bandit: New and Previous Poems*

Shirley Kaufman, *The Floor Keeps Turning*

Shirley Kaufman, *Gold Country*

Abba Kovner, *A Canopy in the Desert*

Larry Levis, *Wrecking Crew*

Belle Randall, *101 Different Ways of Playing Solitaire and Other Poems*

Ed Roberson, *When Thy King Is A Boy*

Dennis Scott, *Uncle Time*

Richard Shelton, *Of All the Dirty Words*

Richard Shelton, *The Tattooed Desert*

David Steingass, *American Handbook*

David Steingass, *Body Compass*

Tomas Tranströmer, *Windows & Stones: Selected Poems*

Marc Weber, *48 Small Poems*

David P. Young, *Sweating Out the Winter*